P9-DHL-592

Contents

Introduction · September 11, 2001

Howell Raines, Executive Editor, *The New York Times*

That bright, blue Tuesday, September 11, was to be a busy day at *The New York Times* newspaper. There was a mayoral primary election to cover, and editors were at their desks early. When word came of the first plane hitting the first tower of the World Trade Center, photographers and reporters raced downtown.

Journalistic instinct and training dictated the initial response, but that day's story was a challenge no one could have predicted in those first minutes. As the hours ticked by, it turned into the tragedy of the World Trade Center, a story of terrorism that forever marked the lives of those who lived through it.

That morning, dozens of reporters and photographers converged on ground zero, Pennsylvania and the Pentagon as others moved out across America, Afghanistan, Pakistan and other crucial locations in Europe, the Middle East and Asia. What made this global crisis different for us at *The Times* is that it happened in our city. It was our story. We lived in the middle of it. *The Times* family lost loved ones. There were reporters here that first day who worked while worrying about where their children or husbands or wives were — or where their families would sleep that night.

But we knew the story was not about us. Our role was to be witnesses and reporters, yet understanding of the emotional pain of our fellow citizens, the rescuers and the survivors and the families who suffered so badly. Our job was to make sure that memories of these days would never go away. This book is a homage to the victims.

It quickly became clear that a story this important required a new approach, some creative way to relate all the events of that one disastrous day. The solution was a new section of the

FRED R. CONRAD/THE NEW YORK TIMES

The twin towers and the Statue of Liberty in 1983.

paper, A Nation Challenged. Introduced one week after September 11, the section gave the newspaper the freedom to show readers the breadth and depth of the story, and it gave us more space for photographs and illustrations. Many of the photographs and illustrations in this book were shown first on the full pages of the section. The digging at ground zero, the anthrax scare, the Qaeda network, Washington's effort to improve domestic security: all were chronicled in great detail on those pages by many of the reporters quoted here. At the end of the section, day after day, ran the Portraits of Grief, close to 2,000 brief stories of the lives of the missing at ground zero. These portraits have become a national shrine.

Looking back, it is easy to put the events of the last months of 2001 in some order. On 9/11, the towers came down. Then the Pentagon was attacked and a fourth plane crashed in the fields of Pennsylvania. Suddenly, the United States was threatened and its people besieged and worried. Mayor Rudolph W. Giuliani of New York became a national symbol of courage as he helped New Yorkers move on with their lives. Soldiers prepared to fight the new enemy. Anthrax seemed to be loose in the mail, killing with a frightening lack of discrimination. And then there really was war.

The pictures and text in this book are a record of our changed world — the world in which this newspaper and its readers live. These photographs show, in the words of the writer James Agee, "the cruel radiance of what is." This book is our tribute to those people who did not live through these last turbulent months: a faithful record of the world they did not live to see.

FRED R. CONRAD/THE NEW YORK TIMES

An old pier next to the Imperial Water Ferry in Hoboken, New Jersey, with the Manhattan skyline in the background. September 13, 2001.

The New York Times

"All the News That's Fit to Print"

VOL. CL... No. 51,874 — NEW YORK, WEDNESDAY, SEPTEMBER 12, 2001 — 75 CENTS

U.S. ATTACKED

HIJACKED JETS DESTROY TWIN TOWERS AND HIT PENTAGON IN DAY OF TERROR

A CREEPING HORROR

Buildings Burn and Fall as Onlookers Search for Elusive Safety

By N. R. KLEINFIELD

President Vows to Exact Punishment for 'Evil'

By SERGE SCHMEMANN

A Somber Bush Says Terrorism Cannot Prevail

By ELISABETH BUMILLER and DAVID E. SANGER

Awaiting the Aftershocks

Washington and Nation Plunge Into Fight With Enemy Hard to Identify and Punish

By R. W. APPLE Jr.

The New York Times

"All the News That's Fit to Print"

VOL. CL... No. 51,875 — NEW YORK, THURSDAY, SEPTEMBER 13, 2001

Late Edition

STUNNED RESCUERS COMB ATTACK SITES, BUT THOUSANDS ARE PRESUMED DEAD; F.B.I. TRACKING HIJACKERS' MOVEMENTS

BIN LADEN TIE CITED

Agents Say They Know Accomplices' Names — Search Is Wide

By DAVID JOHNSTON and JAMES RISEN

A GRIM FORECAST

Barest Count, by Three Hundreds of Firms, Has 1,500 Missing

By ROBERT D. McFADDEN

AFTER THE ATTACKS

Aides Say Bush Was One Target Of Hijacked Jet

A City Awakes, Only to Reflect On a Nightmare

By N. R. KLEINFIELD

On Doomed Flight, Passengers Vowed To Perish Fighting

By JODI WILGOREN and EDWARD WONG

A Few Moments of Hope In a Mountain of Rubble

By DAN BARRY

Pentagon Weighing Plans for Retaliation

The New York Times

"All the News That's Fit to Print"

VOL. CL... No. 51,876 — NEW YORK, FRIDAY, SEPTEMBER 14, 2001 — 75 CENTS

Late Edition

BUSH AND TOP AIDES PROCLAIM POLICY OF 'ENDING' STATES THAT BACK TERROR; LOCAL AIRPORTS SHUT AFTER AN ARREST

9 OTHERS DETAINED

U.S. Says One Had Fake Pilot ID — One Tried to Fly on Tuesday

By CLIFFORD J. LEVY and WILLIAM K. RASHBAUM

President to Visit New York — bin Laden Singled Out

By ELISABETH BUMILLER and JANE PERLEZ

No Middle Ground

By R. W. APPLE Jr.

U.S. Says Hijackers Lived in the Open With Deadly Secret

By KEVIN SACK with DON VAN NATTA Jr.

AFTER THE ATTACKS

Trade Center's Past In a Sad Paper Trail

By JANE FRITSCH and DAVID ROHDE

Seeking New Space, Companies Search Far From Wall St.

By CHARLES V. BAGLI and LESLIE EATON

FLYING THE COLORS

The New York Times

"All the News That's Fit to Print"

VOL. CL... No. 51,877 — NEW YORK, SATURDAY, SEPTEMBER 15, 2001 — 75 CENTS

Late Edition

BUSH LEADS PRAYER, VISITS AID CREWS; CONGRESS BACKS USE OF ARMED FORCE

U.S. Demands Arab Countries 'Choose Sides'

By JANE PERLEZ

A DAY OF MOURNING

President, in New York, Offers Resolute Salute Atop the Rubble

By ROBERT D. McFADDEN

PRESIDENTIAL VISIT Mayor Giuliani and Fire Commissioner Von Essen guided President Bush through the World Trade Center site yesterday.

An Unobtrusive Man's Odyssey: Polite Student to Suicide Hijacker

By STEVE ERLANGER

AFTER THE ATTACKS

Pentagon Tracked Deadly Jet But Found No Way to Stop It

Airlines, in Search of Relief, Warn of Bankruptcy

By LAURENCE ZUCKERMAN

Construction in City Stalled After Attack

1
September 11, 2001

COPYRIGHT © 2001 BY R.O. BLECHMAN

◄ *Front pages of* The New York Times, *September 12–15, 2001.*

Terror Strikes

CARMEN TAYLOR VIA ASSOCIATED PRESS

United Airlines Flight 175 crashes into the south tower at 9:02:54 a.m.

It was one of those moments in which history splits, and we define the world as "before" and "after."

—**Editorial in** *The New York Times*
SEPTEMBER 12, 2001

United Airlines Flight 175, traveling about 480 miles per hour and heavily laden with fuel, struck the south tower between the 78th and 84th floors. American Airlines Flight 11 had already hit the north tower between the 94th and 98th floors at 8:46:26 a.m.

View from East 25th Street, New York City, at 9:58 a.m.

LONNIE SCHLEIN/THE NEW YORK TIMES

Escape From the Towers

Watching the north tower collapse.

ANGEL FRANCO/THE NEW YORK TIMES

On Vesey Street: After escaping the towers, people were not sure which way to run.

RUTH FREMSON/THE NEW YORK TIMES

When the first jet struck 1 World Trade Center at 8:46 a.m. on Tuesday, the people in 2 World Trade Center with a view of the instant inferno across the divide had the clearest sense of what they, too, must do: get out fast.

Without question, particularly at 1 World Trade Center, the north tower, the evacuation of thousands of people went well, with people helping each other with acts of courage great and modest.

People on floors as high as the 88th at the north tower, stepping over rubble, made the full trip to safety. In the packed stairwells, people stepped aside to let burn victims speed past. Firefighters rushed upward, assisting as they climbed.

Port Authority officials say that considerable numbers of people were evacuated within an hour, 30 minutes less than even their drills.

—Michael Moss and Charles V. Bagli
SEPTEMBER 13, 2001

SHANNON STAPLETON/REUTERS

People reaching the base of the north tower.

On an average workday, 35,000 people were in the World Trade Center towers by 9 a.m. On September 11 at 8:46 a.m., each tower held between 5,000 and 7,000 people.

SUZANNE PLUNKETT/ASSOCIATED PRESS

People running from the collapse, down Fulton Street.

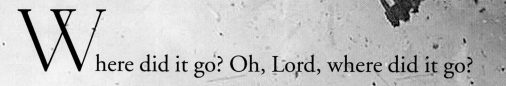

W
here did it go? Oh, Lord, where did it go?

—N.R. Kleinfield
SEPTEMBER 12, 2001

The north tower falls at 10:28 a.m.

CHANG W. LEE/THE NEW YORK TIMES

The Collapse

Published November 11, 2001

Following the attacks, engineers pieced together a likely sequence for the destruction at the World Trade Center.

Anatomy of a Twin Tower

EXTERIOR COLUMNS

They provided about 40 percent of the support for the weight of the building, but their primary purpose was to stiffen the building against the wind.

NORTH ▶

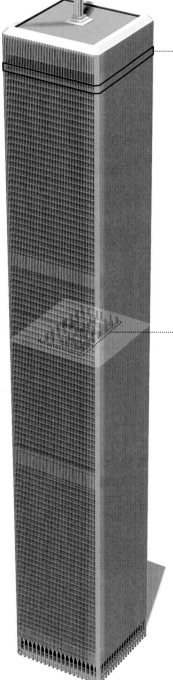

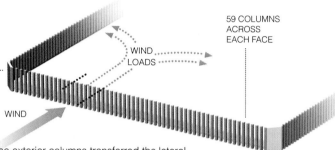

59 COLUMNS ACROSS EACH FACE

WIND LOADS

WIND

The exterior columns transferred the lateral loads from winds through the floors to adjacent walls. There, the loads would be transferred to the ground.

CORE COLUMNS

There were 47 core columns that supported about 60 percent of the building's weight.

FLOOR TRUSSES

The floors were supported by steel trusses. Floor sections were assembled in units, each with six trusses.

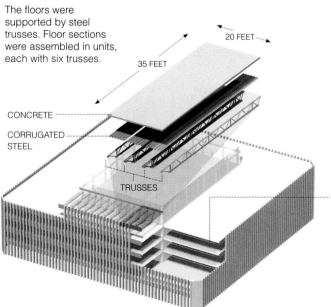

20 FEET

35 FEET

CONCRETE

CORRUGATED STEEL

TRUSSES

FLOORS
The floors also stabilized the vertical columns to prevent buckling.

Published March 29, 2002

Fireproofing, sprinkler systems and the water supply for hoses were all disabled in the twin towers on September 11 in the face of a blaze so intense that it drove temperatures as high as 2,000 degrees and generated heat equivalent to the energy output of a nuclear power plant.

Under normal circumstances, fire suppression systems are designed to allow a high-rise blaze to burn itself out before the building collapses. But on September 11, there were across-the-board failures in the towers' fire suppression systems. The ultimate significance of those failures is extremely difficult to gauge because of the extraordinary circumstances of the attack.

Most of the tenants in the floors below impact, to the credit of the building and the emergency lighting in the stairwells, escaped.

— James Glanz and Eric Lipton

reporting based on a federal study on how the towers fell

Sources: Leslie E. Robertson Associates; Port Authority; Skilling Ward Magnusson Barkshire; Dr. Yogesh Jaluria, Rutgers University; Dr. Eduardo Kausel, M.I.T.; Dr. Tomasz Wierzbicki, M.I.T.; International Federation of Air Line Dispatchers' Associations

Why the North Tower Fell

Though the two towers did not collapse in exactly the same way, a detailed look at the collapse of the north tower sheds light on the crucial elements of both collapses.

NORTH ►

98

IMPACT
AREA   94

THE COLLISION WITH THE TOWER

At 8:46 a.m., a Boeing 767 with nearly 10,000 gallons of fuel onboard hits the north face, exerting a force equivalent to about 25 million pounds. A huge explosion and fire ensue.

AMERICAN
AIRLINES
FLIGHT 11

THE COLUMNS

The impact causes severe structural damage, blowing out some 35 exterior columns between floors 94 and 98 and obliterating portions of those floors. The impact also knocks loose some fireproofing on the columns and trusses.

About a third of the impact's energy is spent before pieces of the plane strike the core columns. Calculations suggest that no more than half of the core columns are seriously damaged.

LIKE AN ARCH

Columns and beams near the damaged area begin to function like an arch, transferring loads around the hole and downward through remaining columns at the sides. The building stands for 102 minutes, giving many people a chance to escape.

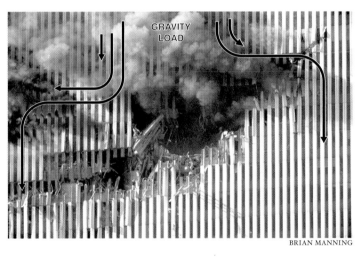

GRAVITY
LOAD

BRIAN MANNING

Meanwhile, though, heat from the burning fuel and other materials raises temperatures to more than 1,100 degrees, the point at which steel begins losing its strength. Nearly 40,000 tons of building weight sit within and above the impact area.

THE FALL

❶ The steel trusses are particularly vulnerable to the fire because their ratio of surface area to volume is large, causing them to heat up quickly. Extreme heat softens the steel and reduces its ability to support the floors.

❷ Having lost their lateral support, the exterior columns, already softened by the fire, buckle catastrophically.

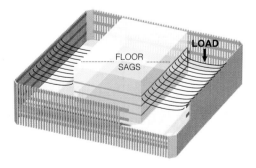

FLOOR
SAGS

LOAD

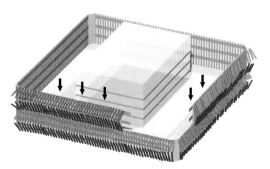

As the floors weaken, they tug at their connections, which tear away from the core and exterior columns.

The top portion of the building plummets, and the building collapses in roughly 12 seconds. A stone dropped from the top of the tower would have taken 9.2 seconds to fall to the ground.

STEVE DUENES AND MIKA GRÖNDAHL/THE NEW YORK TIMES

17

Heroic Response

KRISTA NILES/THE NEW YORK TIMES

Firefighters from Ladder 21 embrace a colleague who cannot find a family member, who is also a firefighter.

Shaken firefighters and officers spent much of the day searching through the rubble for lost colleagues, mourning and rearranging responsibilities as they attempted to deal with the loss of so many senior people.

—Kevin Flynn
SEPTEMBER 13, 2001

Firefighters work amid the debris from 7 World Trade Center. ▶

TING-LI WANG/THE NEW YORK TIMES

Hundreds of firefighters gather at the scene immediately after the collapse of the towers to help in any way they can.

JUSTIN LANE FOR THE NEW YORK TIMES

Treating the Survivors

At West Broadway and Chambers Street, an emergency worker treats a man hurt in the attack.

CHANG W. LEE/THE NEW YORK TIMES

At hospitals throughout Lower Manhattan, hundreds of doctors and nurses worked as though all part of one big MASH unit, tending to the wounded at the front lines of a war. Meanwhile, many of those who had not been injured — at least not physically — by the worst terrorist attack in American history donated the only thing they could think of, their blood.

—**Dan Barry**
SEPTEMBER 12, 2001

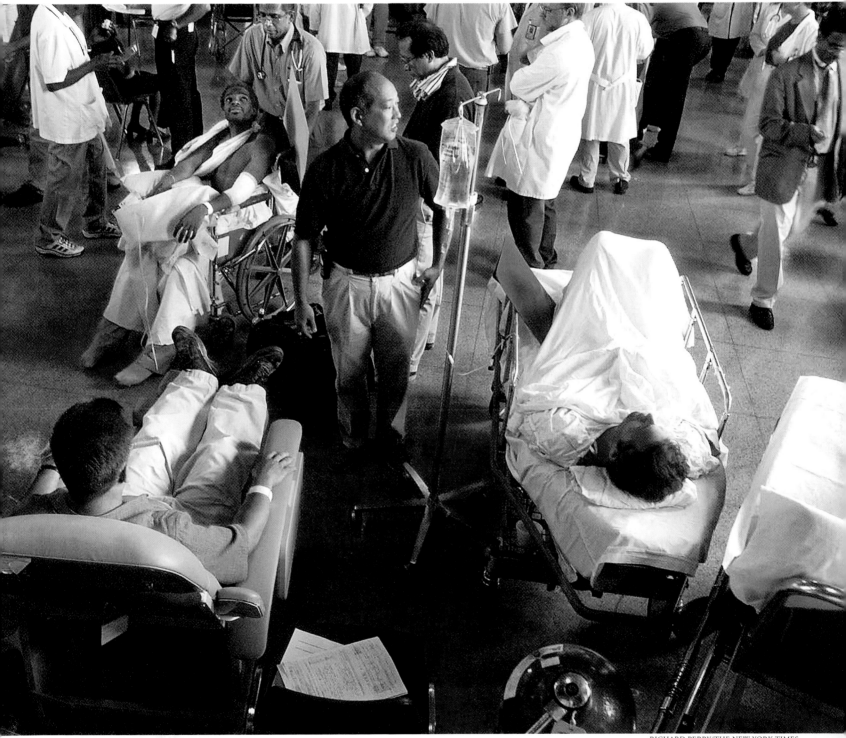

RICHARD PERRY/THE NEW YORK TIMES

The hospital auditorium at Jersey City Medical Center is turned into a treatment center for those who sustained minor injuries in the attack on the World Trade Center.

23

Attack on the Pentagon

PAUL HOSEFROS/THE NEW YORK TIMES

On September 11 at 9:37 a.m., American Airlines Flight 77 crashed into the Pentagon, one of the world's most secure military installations.

Many of the Pentagon's more than 20,000 civilians and military workers were already on edge when the attack came. News of the crashes at the trade center had shot through the corridors and it seemed as if every office television was turned on. Military and civilian employees watched in disbelief as smoke engulfed the two towers.

Foreshadowing what then happened, Mike Slater, a former Marine, told his coworkers, "We're next."

Then the Pentagon, built to withstand terrorist attacks, shook like a rickety roller coaster. A section of it collapsed and burned. "It sounded like a roar," said Mr. Slater, who was 500 yards away from where the jet slammed into the Pentagon's west side. "I knew it was a bomb or something."

—**Don van Natta and Lizette Alvarez**
SEPTEMBER 12, 2001

> The Pentagon is virtually a city in itself. Approximately 23,000 people work there. More than 200,000 telephone calls are made daily through phones connected by 100,000 miles of telephone cable.

Fires continued to burn in the western side of the Pentagon on September 12, but more than half of the offices were open.

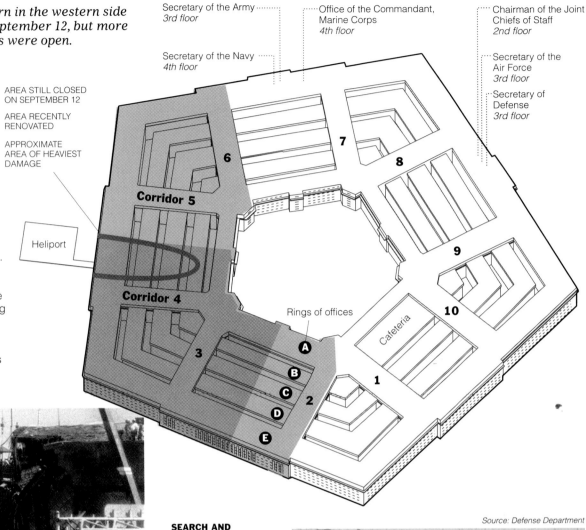

Secretary of the Army ....
3rd floor

Secretary of the Navy ....
4th floor

Office of the Commandant,
Marine Corps
4th floor

Chairman of the Joint
Chiefs of Staff
2nd floor

Secretary of the
Air Force
3rd floor

Secretary of
Defense
3rd floor

▨ AREA STILL CLOSED
ON SEPTEMBER 12

▨ AREA RECENTLY
RENOVATED

APPROXIMATE
AREA OF HEAVIEST
DAMAGE

THE DAMAGE

Part of the outermost ring collapsed completely, and the worst damage extended into the first and second floors of the B-ring.

Heliport

THE FIRES

Fire officials said they were having difficulty penetrating the slate roof to reach the areas still burning on September 12, but by evening, they said the fires were under control.

Corridor 5

Corridor 4

6

7

8

9

10

Rings of offices

Cafeteria

3

Ⓐ

Ⓑ

Ⓒ

2

Ⓓ

Ⓔ

1

SUSANA RAAB FOR THE NEW YORK TIMES

A row of F.B.I. agents search for plane debris on the lawn outside the Pentagon on September 12.

SEARCH AND RESCUE EFFORTS

A total of four 60-member search and rescue teams arrived from Fairfax and Montgomery counties, Virginia; Virginia Beach; and Tennessee. They were assisted by a military engineering company and firefighters from several states.

Source: Defense Department

PENNSYLVANIA AVE.

K ST.

VIRGINIA AVE.

12TH ST.

N. CAPITOL ST.

G ST.

White House

Washington

State Dept.

CONSTITUTION AVE.

Capitol

66

THE MALL

INDEPENDENCE AVE.

110

Tidal
Basin

SEVENTH ST.

395

ARLINGTON
NATIONAL
CEMETERY

27

M ST.

The Pentagon

395

233

Potomac
River

Anacostia
River

VIRGINIA

1

RONALD REAGAN
WASHINGTON
NATIONAL AIRPORT

THE NEW YORK TIMES

The Crash in Pennsylvania

A United Airlines flight bound from Newark to San Francisco plunged into a grassy field outside the mining town of Shanksville, Pennsylvania [at 10:06 a.m.], about an hour after the attack on the World Trade Center.

The crash came minutes after a passenger reportedly called an emergency dispatcher from his cell phone and said that the plane had been hijacked and was "going down."

—Jere Longman and Sara Rimer
SEPTEMBER 12, 2001

They told the people they loved that they would die fighting.

In a series of cellular telephone calls to their wives, two passengers aboard the plane that crashed into a Pennsylvania field instead of possibly toppling a national landmark learned about the horror of the World Trade Center. From 35,000 feet, they relayed harrowing details about the hijacking in progress to the police. And they vowed to try to thwart the enemy, to prevent others from dying even if they could not save themselves.

The accounts revealed a spirit of defiance amid the desperation. Relatives and friends and a congressman who represents the area around the crash site in Pennsylvania hailed the fallen passengers as the patriots of America's darkest day.

"Apparently they made enough of a difference that the plane did not complete its mission," said Lyzbeth Glick's [passenger Jeremy Glick's widow] uncle, Tom Crowley, of Atlanta. In an e-mail message forwarded far and wide, Mr. Crowley urged: "May we remember Jeremy and the other brave souls as heroes, soldiers and Americans on United Flight 93 who so gallantly gave their lives to save many others."

—Jodi Wilgoren and Edward Wong
SEPTEMBER 13, 2001

DAVID LLOYD/TRIBUNE-DEMOCRAT VIA ASSOCIATED PRESS

Firefighters and emergency personnel at the scene of the crash of United Airlines Flight 93, about 80 miles southeast of Pittsburgh, Pennsylvania.

Morning of Destruction

By 8 a.m. on September 11, a chain of events had been set in motion that, two hours later, would erase the World Trade Center towers from the New York City skyline, rip open the west wall of the Pentagon, drop four planes from the sky and kill 3,047 people. Following is a look at how events unfolded. All times are Eastern Daylight.

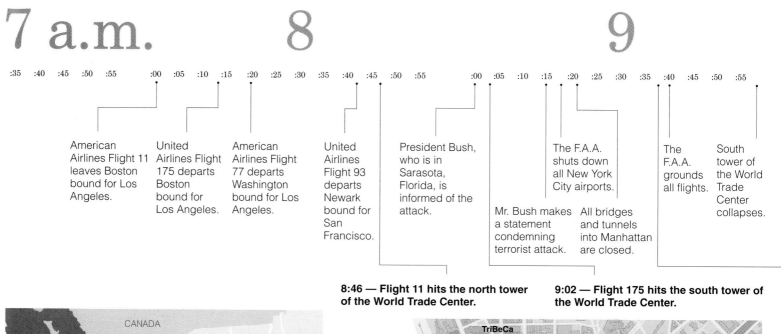

7 a.m.   8   9

:35 :40 :45 :50 :55   :00 :05 :10 :15 :20 :25 :30 :35 :40 :45 :50 :55   :00 :05 :10 :15 :20 :25 :30 :35 :40 :45 :50 :55

American Airlines Flight 11 leaves Boston bound for Los Angeles.

United Airlines Flight 175 departs Boston bound for Los Angeles.

American Airlines Flight 77 departs Washington bound for Los Angeles.

United Airlines Flight 93 departs Newark bound for San Francisco.

President Bush, who is in Sarasota, Florida, is informed of the attack.

Mr. Bush makes a statement condemning terrorist attack.

The F.A.A. shuts down all New York City airports.

All bridges and tunnels into Manhattan are closed.

The F.A.A. grounds all flights.

South tower of the World Trade Center collapses.

8:46 — Flight 11 hits the north tower of the World Trade Center.

9:02 — Flight 175 hits the south tower of the World Trade Center.

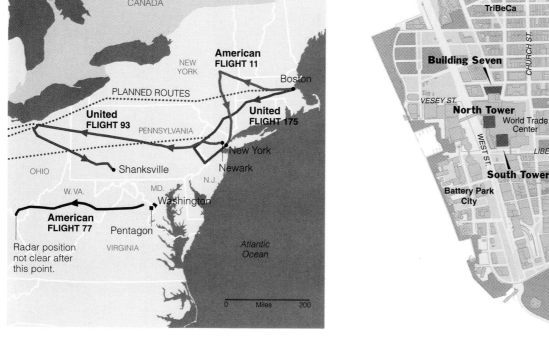

CANADA

NEW YORK

American FLIGHT 11

Boston

PLANNED ROUTES

United FLIGHT 93

PENNSYLVANIA

United FLIGHT 175

New York

OHIO   Shanksville

Newark

N.J.

W. VA.   MD.

Washington

American FLIGHT 77   Pentagon

VIRGINIA   Atlantic Ocean

Radar position not clear after this point.

0   Miles   200

TriBeCa

MANHATTAN

City Hall

Building Seven

CHURCH ST.

BROOKLYN BRIDGE

VESEY ST.

North Tower

World Trade Center

FULTON ST.

WEST ST.

LIBERTY ST.

MAIDEN LA.

South Tower

BROADWAY

WALL ST.

Battery Park City

Financial District

28

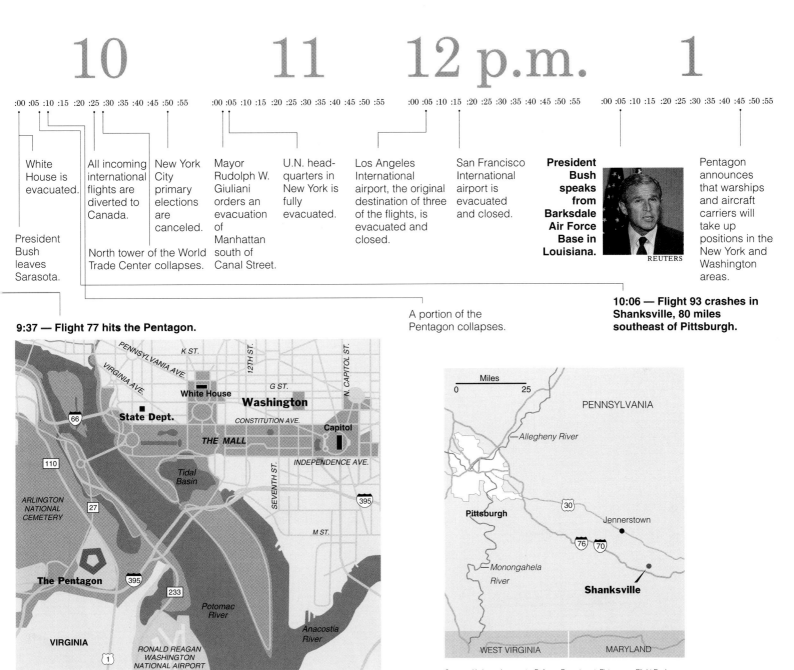

10   11   12 p.m.   1

:00 :05 :10 :15 :20 :25 :30 :35 :40 :45 :50 :55   :00 :05 :10 :15 :20 :25 :30 :35 :40 :45 :50 :55   :00 :05 :10 :15 :20 :25 :30 :35 :40 :45 :50 :55   :00 :05 :10 :15 :20 :25 :30 :35 :40 :45 :50 :55

White House is evacuated.

All incoming international flights are diverted to Canada.

New York City primary elections are canceled.

Mayor Rudolph W. Giuliani orders an evacuation of Manhattan south of Canal Street.

U.N. head-quarters in New York is fully evacuated.

Los Angeles International airport, the original destination of three of the flights, is evacuated and closed.

San Francisco International airport is evacuated and closed.

President Bush speaks from Barksdale Air Force Base in Louisiana.

REUTERS

Pentagon announces that warships and aircraft carriers will take up positions in the New York and Washington areas.

President Bush leaves Sarasota.

North tower of the World Trade Center collapses.

9:37 — Flight 77 hits the Pentagon.

A portion of the Pentagon collapses.

10:06 — Flight 93 crashes in Shanksville, 80 miles southeast of Pittsburgh.

Washington map

PENNSYLVANIA AVE.
K ST.
VIRGINIA AVE.
12TH ST.
N. CAPITOL ST.
White House
G ST.
Washington
66
State Dept.
CONSTITUTION AVE.
Capitol
THE MALL
INDEPENDENCE AVE.
110
SEVENTH ST.
Tidal Basin
395
M ST.
ARLINGTON NATIONAL CEMETERY
27
The Pentagon
395
233
Potomac River
Anacostia River
VIRGINIA
1
RONALD REAGAN WASHINGTON NATIONAL AIRPORT

Pennsylvania map

Miles
0   25
PENNSYLVANIA
Allegheny River
30
Pittsburgh
Jennerstown
76 70
Monongahela River
Shanksville
WEST VIRGINIA   MARYLAND

Sources: Various wire reports; Defense Department; Flytecomm; Flight Explorer

29

Eyewitnesses

"I Heard the Plane"

NATALIA LESZ, *a 21-year-old student staying in a hotel in Union Square while her apartment was being renovated, was on the phone with her mother in Warsaw:*
"I called my mom at 9 a.m. and was talking about a guy I met. I speak to my mother every morning. Then my dog, Izzy, a Maltese, raised his head. I heard the plane in the seventh floor of the W hotel. I told her 'I think a plane is next to my window.'"

Barclay Street near West Broadway

First Plane Hits

GREGORY DOWNER *was walking his dog at Fifth Avenue and 11th Street:*
"There were 12 people. We all looked up. We all thought it would be unusual for a plane to be flying so low over the city.

"It scooped down even lower over the South Village — almost like a missile — and then toward the north tower of the World Trade Center. When it went into the building we all screamed — we couldn't believe what we saw."

The Brooklyn Bridge

LYNN SIMPSON, *communications director of Strategic Communications Group, was on the 89th floor of 1 World Trade Center:*
"I heard an enormous crash. The ceiling fell in, the lights went out and the sprinklers went on. There was a fire in the stairwell. I told everyone to get out.
"We went into a side office and we were listening to the radio — some talk show — and the D.J.s were joking, saying a kamikaze pilot has crashed into the World Trade Center and they were laughing. We thought we were going to die."

Between Crashes

SHARNISE WINGATE, *25, a telephone service technician for Verizon, was making a repair call in Brooklyn Heights when a friend called her to tell her that one of the towers had been hit:*

"I was watching the flames and saw a second aircraft come in low and make a sharp left into the second tower. I was confused. It didn't look like a rescue aircraft."

In front of Trinity Church

Towers Collapse

KEITH VANCE, *33, was standing on Broadway in front of Trinity Church when he saw the tower collapse:*

"I was surprised how long it lasted. It was probably only 30 seconds, but it felt like five minutes."

Beyond the Blast

MALKIE YADAIE, *the owner of Ben-Ness Photos on University Place, said that people rushed in to buy disposable cameras:*

"Some didn't wait for their change, just ran out. Some were screaming."

Victims and Rescuers

THE REV. LLOYD PRATOR *stood on the sidewalk to meet the ambulances to bless victims and give last rites:*

"It was a glimpse of hell. People were covered with debris and glass. Everyone was covered with ash."

Stage Door Deli on Vesey Street

Staying Strong

President George W. Bush addresses the nation. September 11, 2001.

DOUG MILLS/ASSOCIATED PRESS

President Bush, in his initial talk to the nation, expressed his desire that the country show the perpetrators that it cannot be brought down by terrorism. Psychological experts agree that it is important to resume normal life as soon as possible.

—Jane E. Brody
SEPTEMBER 18, 2001

POOL PHOTO BY ROBERT F. BUKATY

Mayor Rudolph W. Giuliani, center, leads Senator Charles Schumer of New York, second from left, Governor George E. Pataki of New York, second from right, and Senator Hillary Rodham Clinton of New York, right, on a tour of the site. September 12, 2001.

These acts shattered steel, but they cannot dent the steel of American resolve.

—**President George W. Bush**
SEPTEMBER 12, 2001

33

CHESTER HIGGINS JR./THE NEW YORK TIMES

2
The Days After

◄ *A makeshift shrine in Union Square
Park, New York. September 17, 2001.*

FRED R. CONRAD/THE NEW YORK TIMES

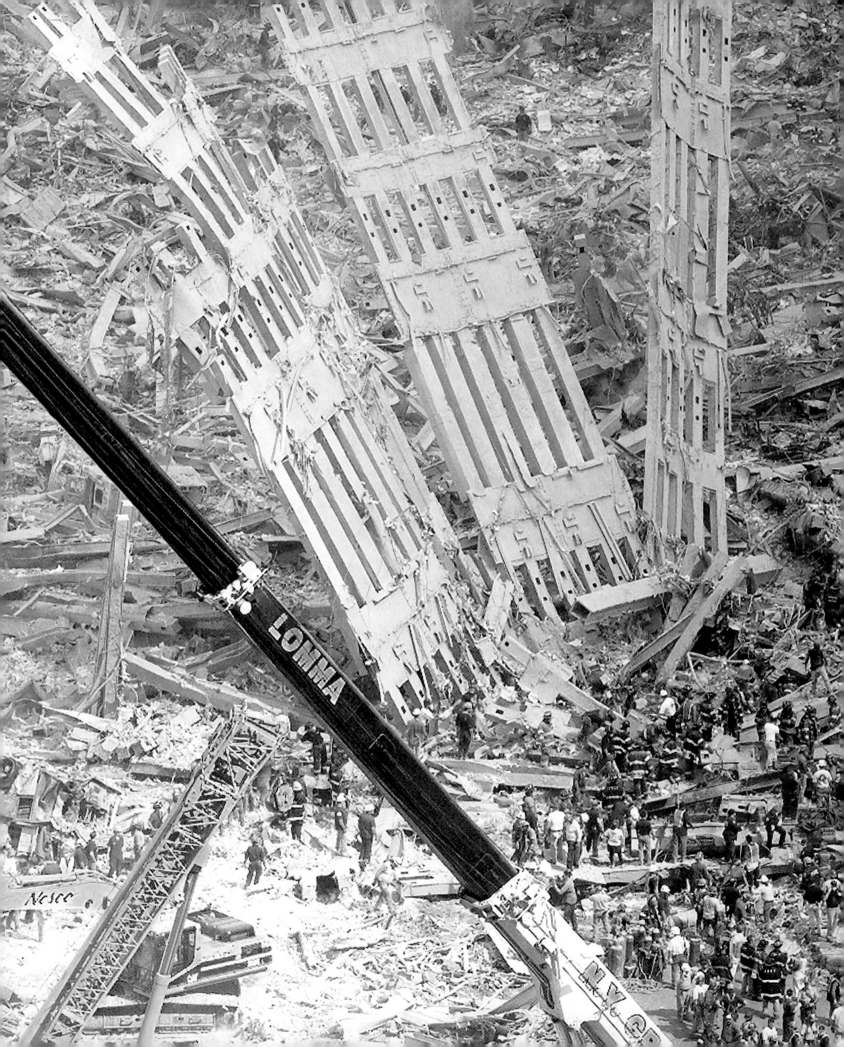

By late afternoon, the jaws of huge cranes were biting indiscriminately into the piles of rubble, while police officers, firefighters, soldiers and other rescue workers pried at the ground with shovels and crowbars.

—**Dan Barry**
SEPTEMBER 13, 2001

Hundreds of emergency workers continue rescue efforts amid the wreckage of the World Trade Center. September 12, 2001.

RUTH FREMSON/THE NEW YORK TIMES

The New Cityscape

September 10, 2001.

September 11, 2001.

PHOTOGRAPHS BY DENTON TILLMAN

"There's no way an amateur could have, with any degree of reliability, done what was done yesterday," John Nance [an airline pilot, author and aviation analyst] said.

—**James Glanz**
SEPTEMBER 13, 2001

A satellite photo of Manhattan, taken on September 12, 2001. ▶

U.S. GEOLOGICAL SURVEY

Heartfelt Donations

Donations sit along 14th Street in front of a Salvation Army office. The inside of the building is full. September 15, 2001.

F rom the $4.37 that a 4-year-old girl emptied out of her Pokémon wallet to a $10 million pledge from the Starr Foundation, donations small and large flowed into New York.

A group of doctors and nurses who drove up from Kentucky left six plastic bins filled with latex gloves, surgical gloves and other medical supplies. The bins sat lined up on the sidewalk, next to garbage bags filled with shoes and secondhand clothing. Nearby, emergency service workers on their way downtown scooped granola bars and bagels off a folding stretcher, which served as a counter.

New Yorkers arrived at Chelsea Piers, the Jacob K. Javits Convention Center and other drop-off points by foot, bicycle, pickup truck and leather-seated Range Rover, depositing bags of ice from the meatpacking district, shopping carts full of socks and underwear from Kmart, and peanut butter and jelly sandwiches they had prepared at home.

More than 30 major charities have collected at least $1.4 billion in aid for the families of the victims of September 11. As of March 11, 2002, the Red Cross raised $930 million to aid September 11 victims and distributed $558 million.

—**Elissa Gootman**
SEPTEMBER 14, 2001

DITH PRAN/THE NEW YORK TIMES

An army of volunteers helps move supplies from the waterfront of Jersey City, New Jersey, to the rescue operation in Lower Manhattan. September 15, 2001.

New York's cup is running over. From every state in the union and from just about every continent, donated goods and volunteers have been rolling into the city, out of the goodness of millions of hearts. Many of these efforts were launched after announcements that some commodities were needed; underwear, for instance, or work gloves, both of which are now in ample supply. They are a balm to a city aching with loss, and also to people who make the offerings.

—**Jim Dwyer**
SEPTEMBER 16, 2001

41

Leaders Take Action

President Bush, center, Mayor Rudolph W. Giuliani, left, Governor George E. Pataki, second from left, Senator Charles Schumer, third from right, and Fire Commissioner Thomas Van Essen, right, look toward the fallen buildings. September 14, 2001.

DOUG MILLS/ASSOCIATED PRESS

Mr. Giuliani was more than just a mayor. Day after day, his calm explanation of complicated, awful news helped to reassure a traumatized city that it would pull through, and that someone was in charge. He attended funerals, comforted survivors, urged residents to dine out and tourists to come in, all the while exuding compassion and resolve, even as the new threat of anthrax emerged. He was now being greeted with cheers wherever he went: Rudy! Rudy! Rudy!

— **Dan Barry**
DECEMBER 31, 2001

LIBRADO ROMERO/THE NEW YORK TIMES

Members of the armed services stand guard along Chambers Street in New York City to keep the area clear for rescue workers. September 12, 2001.

ANGEL FRANCO/THE NEW YORK TIMES

Today [Bush] said the attacks "were more than acts of terror; they were acts of war," a distinction intended to lay the groundwork for military action.

—Katharine Q. Seelye and Elisabeth Bumiller
SEPTEMBER 13, 2001

The National Guard checks the ID of a Wall Street worker. September 17, 2001.

43

Search for the Missing

KRISTA NILES/THE NEW YORK TIMES

At Bellevue Hospital, a wall becomes a billboard for posters of some of the thousands of people still missing. September 13, 2001.

As of May 30, 2002, 2,823 people from more than 115 countries were listed as having died in the attacks on the World Trade Center. Of those, 147 people were on the two hijacked planes that crashed into the towers.

At the Pentagon, 184 people died, with 59 dead on the hijacked plane.

In Pennsylvania, 40 people died on the hijacked plane.

People post fliers across New York City seeking news of missing loved ones. September 13, 2001. ▶

NICOLE BENGIVENO/THE NEW YORK TIMES

A Time to Mourn

A candlight vigil on the Lower East Side of Manhattan on the evening of September 12, 2001.

ANDREA MOHIN/THE NEW YORK TIMES

The city will survive because New York is too big and too ornery to do anything else. But for the moment, this great city grieves.

—**Bob Herbert**
Op-Ed page
SEPTEMBER 13, 2001

CLOCKWISE FROM UPPER LEFT: RUTH FREMSON/THE NEW YORK TIMES, JAMES ESTRIN/THE NEW YORK TIMES, STEVE BERMAN/THE NEW YORK TIMES, KEVIN P. COUGHLIN FOR THE NEW YORK TIMES, RUTH FREMSON/THE NEW YORK TIMES, CHESTER HIGGINS JR./THE NEW YORK TIMES, OZIER MUHAMMAD/THE NEW YORK TIMES

The World Grieves

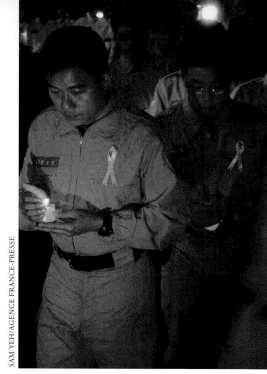

SAM YEH/AGENCE FRANCE-PRESSE

Taipei, Taiwan

Nairobi, Kenya

KAREL PRINSLOO/ASSOCIATED PRESS

This week, "we are all New Yorkers."

—**R.W. Apple Jr.**
*quoting Dominique Moisu, French
scholar on international affairs*
SEPTEMBER 14, 2001

Southeastern University in Davie, Florida

ROBERT MAYER/SOUTH FLORIDA SUN-SENTINEL

Los Angeles, California

MONICA ALMEIDA/THE NEW YORK TIMES

London, England

POOL PHOTO BY MAX NASH

Bhopal, India

REUTERS

49

The Lost Brothers

Four of the five members of Engine Company 226 in Brooklyn Heights who went out from this firehouse on September 11 never returned. September 13, 2001.

NANCY SIESEL/THE NEW YORK TIMES

A total of 343 firefighters, nearly 30 times the number ever lost by the department in a single event, were killed in the attack. The dead included five of the department's most senior officials, including the chief who specialized in directing rescues from collapses of this sort. Also buried in the rubble: 91 fire trucks. The department pushed through promotions and accelerated hiring and, numerically, is back to full strength. But the loss of experience and the emotional hurt remain deeply felt throughout the ranks.

—**Kevin Flynn**
MARCH 21, 2002

The firehouse on Eighth Avenue and 47th Street, known as the Pride of Midtown, is home to Engine Company 54, Ladder Company 4 and Battalion 9, which together lost 15 firefighters. September 14, 2001. ▶

SUZANNE DECHILLO/THE NEW YORK TIMES

In Memoriam

The funeral of an EMS worker at Mount Hope
Cemetery. September 14, 2001.

GEORGE M. GUTIERREZ FOR THE NEW YORK TIMES

Firefighters give a blessing at the funeral of Mychal F. Judge,
the Franciscan Friar who was Chaplain of the Fire
Department of New York City. September 15, 2001.

SUZANNE DECHILLO/THE NEW YORK TIMES

ANGEL FRANCO/THE NEW YORK TIMES

Policemen at the funeral of Dominick Pezzulo, a Port Authority officer. September 19, 2001.

NANCY SIESEL/THE NEW YORK TIMES

The funeral of Firefighter Durrell Pearsall of Rescue 4. November 9, 2001.

53

Letters From Children

Following September 11, *The New York Times* received thousands of letters and drawings from children around the world. Here are a few.

Dear New York
I woke up at 5am 12/09/01. Here in New Zealand it was already your tomorrow. I heard my Mum crying and when I saw what was happening to you I thought it was a horrible dream or bad movie. That day lots of people were crying and still are. On that day it was very quiet at school and noone laughed or ate much lunch. People go to church and meet in public places to pray and light some candles for you.

New Zealand is along way away isn't it. How can I make it better for you. I am only ten and haven't got alot of money. I feel like my own family has been hurt. I am proud of you because you are so brave and will fight back. My Grandad used to be a Policeman and I would never want to live without him in my life. I know that some of your families have lost Policemen Dads and Grandfathers. They are heroes to you and me.

I want to tell the children in your city that the children in New Zealand really care about you. I do and I am praying for you that you will be safe. God really listens to childrens prayers. Pray to him for help and to feel strong and safe. Sometimes bad things happen but God is very wise and strong. He'll help you fix it. One day I will visit your beautiful country and see New York, my Dad has been there.

Love from Bobby Franklin
Christchurch
New Zealand

I woke up at 5am 12/09/01. Here in New Zealand it was already your tomorrow. I heard my Mum crying and when I saw what was happening to you I thought it was a horrible dream or bad movie….On that day it was very quiet at school and noone [sic] laughed or ate much lunch. People go to church and meet in public places to pray and light some candles for you.

New Zealand is along [sic] way away isn't it. How can I make it better for you. I am only ten and haven't got alot [sic] of money. I feel like my own family has been hurt….

I want to tell the children in your city that the children in New Zealand really care about you. I do and I am praying for you that you will be safe. God really listens to childrens [sic] prayers.

Bobby Franklin
Christchurch, New Zealand

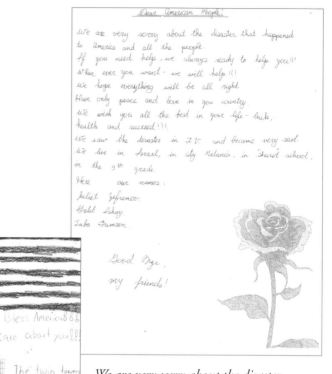

The flag means to me that people care about us so we can have freedom. I think that red stands for the blood people have to loose [sic] for our freedom, white stands for the clean friendship between our friend [sic], and blue stands [sic] our fresh blue sky….I feel so sad….You are in are [sic] prayers….I hope this letter will mean something to you.

Name Unknown

We are very sorry about the disaster that happened to America and all the people….We saw the disaster in T.V. [sic] and became very sad. We live in Israel, in city [sic] Natania, in "sharet" school, in the 9th grade.

Juliet Yefremov
Galit Ishay
Luba Fumson
Natania, Israel

54

I'm proud to be an American. Thank you for all you are doing.

Shamari Wilson, student
Donna Francis, teacher
Deaf Education, Jefferson Elementary, Sherman, Texas

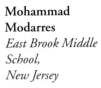

Mohammad Modarres
East Brook Middle School, New Jersey

The New York Times
229 west 43rd street
New York NY 10036

To whom it may concern, I am writing this letter to show the sorrow, and pain that I feel for all of the people how have died, and the families of those how have perished because of this tragedy.

My name is Emily McCoy, I am a 14 year old freshman attending Arcata High school in northern California. In all my wildest dreams I never thought anything of this magnitude would ever happen, not in my lifetime, or ever. We the people of the United States must stick together in this time of need. There will always be people with bad inside of them, and they can't be changed. Something like this never has a humane reason behind it, and it never will.

We like so many other countries in this world, full of loving, caring people, are smart enough to find the right way out of this. If we are to strike back like this, killing more innocent people, that would just make us the ignorant humans and in the end, that it's self is what will kill all mankind off. The bullies, never makes the right choices, and in the long run will only get themselves into more trouble. To be a strong country we need to be smart, and keep things under control, protecting our leaders, and saving our souls.

Truthfully yours,
Emily McCoy
Emily McCoy

New York Times Newspaper
New York City, New York
Sept.13/01

Dear Editor,
please pass this on to the people
of New York. This is Tyler weinkauf
and Joel Gagne from Macklin,
Saskatchewan, Canada.
We are also sorry to hear
the tragedy of lost lives
in New York City. We can't donate
blood or give any money, but we
hope you find more survivors. So here is

To whom it may concern, I am writing this letter to show the sorrow, and pain that I feel. . . . In all my wildest dreams I never thought anything of this magnitude would ever happen, not in my lifetime, or ever. We the people of the United States must stick together in this time of need.

Emily McCoy
Arcata High School, California

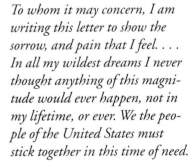

We are also [sic] sorry to hear the tragedy of lost lives in New York City. We can't donate blood or give any money, but we hope you find more survivors. So here is a letter to you. We hope and pray for you and your families and friends who have lost loved ones. . . . We are proud of the fireman [sic] and police who put their lives on the line.

Tyler Weinkauf and Joel Gagné
On behalf of the Macklin 5/6 class, Saskatchewan, Canada

Jessica M.

Remembering the Lost

A mural at O'Brien Street and Soundview in the Bronx was painted to honor the victims of the terrorist attacks. September 19, 2001.

New Yorkers were members of a tribe in shock, tied in knots and easily moved to sudden tears and swift kindnesses. People moved through Midtown without the ordinary get-out-of-my-way pace. They listened to radios. They grabbed one-minute updates from strangers. They spoke urgently into cell phones. They waited quietly in long lines — no shoving, no impatient words — at the pay phones on street corners. The hundreds who sat or stood under outdoor jumbo electronic television screens were virtually silent; it was no time for small talk.

— Jim Dwyer and Susan Sachs
SEPTEMBER 12, 2001

NICOLE BENGIVENO/THE NEW YORK TIMES

People place flowers and other items along a fence in Washington Square Park in New York City. September 13, 2001.

POOL PHOTO BY EARNIE GRAFTON

3
Meeting the Challenge
Abroad

◄ *Marines at the Kandahar airport in Afghanistan, after the defeat of the Taliban. December 26, 2001.*

JAMES HILL FOR THE NEW YORK TIMES

Going to War

PHOTOGRAPHS BY STEPHEN CROWLEY/THE NEW YORK TIMES

A crew member moves out of the way as a fighter jet takes off from the deck of the U.S.S. Theodore Roosevelt. Off Norfolk, Virginia. September 19, 2001.

Today, more than 50,000 American soldiers, sailors, airmen and marines are deployed across a region stretching from the Red Sea to the Indian Ocean, Pentagon officials said. Thousands more are expected to join the effort along with still more warplanes and other material in still more countries surrounding Afghanistan.

Roughly half of the total American forces — about 25,000 — are aboard naval vessels operating in the northern Arabian Sea.

More than 400 American aircraft — including sea- and land-based fighter jets and long-range bombers — are already flying scores of combat missions a day, supported by reconnaissance aircraft, cargo jets and aerial refuelers in elaborately choreographed operations.

In addition, nearly two dozen American ships are operating in the North Arabian Sea, including nuclear-powered submarines, an amphibious assault group carrying the 15th Marine Expeditionary Unit and two aircraft carriers, the Theodore Roosevelt and the Carl Vinson. A third carrier, the Kitty Hawk, is also in the area, carrying an undisclosed number of Special Operations helicopters and soldiers.

—**Michael R. Gordon**
NOVEMBER 8, 2001

When the call to mobilize her Army Reserve unit came on Monday night, Jaimie Strathmeyer was at home in the apartment she shares with Keith Kravitz, their 14-month-old son, Kody, Mr. Kravitz's 7-year-old daughter, Shaiyann, and two pet snakes. This weekend, their household will be dissolved — Kody packed off to Ms. Strathmeyer's parents in Lancaster County and Shaiyann to her mother; the apartment cleaned out and abandoned; the snakes placed in a new home, still to be chosen.

And on Tuesday morning, Specialist Strathmeyer, Sergeant Kravitz and the rest of the 367 Military Police Company will be joining their units. As a soldier, Ms. Strathmeyer is proud to be serving her country. "I know it will be an adventure and an experience," she said.

"I joined the Reserves four years ago, when I was still in high school," she said. "I wasn't a mom yet, so there was no way to know how this would feel. It's not easy to turn your whole life upside down in a matter of moments, and say good-bye to a toddler."

Across the nation, as reservists in every branch of the armed services are called to duty for up to two years, this is a time of wrenching goodbyes and rearranged lives.

U.S. soldiers went to Afghanistan to fight the Taliban and Al Qaeda. The Taliban controlled Afghanistan's government and forced the citizens to follow very harsh rules, according to its interpretation of the Koran. (For example, no one could watch television or play music; girls could not go to school and women could not have jobs.) Al Qaeda is an international terrorist group, founded by Osama bin Laden, that gave money and support to the Taliban. In exchange, the Taliban allowed Al Qaeda to train terrorists and plan attacks from a secure base in Afghanistan. Al Qaeda members believe that all people should adopt their radically orthodox interpretation of the Koran. They consider the U.S. and other Western countries the enemy of Islam. Al Qaeda members carry out terrorist attacks to further their cause.

—Tamar Lewin
OCTOBER 7, 2001

A sailor approaches the U.S.S. Theodore Roosevelt. Norfolk, Virginia. September 19, 2001.

The Qaeda Network

*Osama bin Laden in
Afghanistan, April 1998*

To the United States government, the 44-year-old Saudi exile is the most wanted fugitive in history, the founder and leader of a terrorist network known as Al Qaeda (The Base), which has in a decade trained [many thousands of] militants in Sudan and Afghanistan and posted them to perhaps 50 countries to await their turn to strike. And strike they have, American officials assert, with bin Laden plans, money or inspiration behind the bombings of the trade center in 1993 (6 dead), two American embassies in Africa in 1998 (224 dead) and the destroyer Cole in Yemen in 2000 (17 dead), and the jetliners that collapsed the trade center towers, damaged the Pentagon and crashed in Pennsylvania on September 11 [several thousands feared dead].

To millions of Americans, who have seen his face on television daily and on magazine covers and front pages of newspapers, Mr. bin Laden is the mask of evil; in many minds he is already guilty of killing thousands, although he has not been found, let alone tried.

—**Robert D. McFadden**
SEPTEMBER 30, 2001

Anatomy of a Mountain Bunker

Some of the man-made burrows deep inside mountains in Afghanistan were upgraded by Al Qaeda in recent years. Roomier and with more amenities than naturally formed caves, bunkers like this may have housed Osama bin Laden and his soldiers.

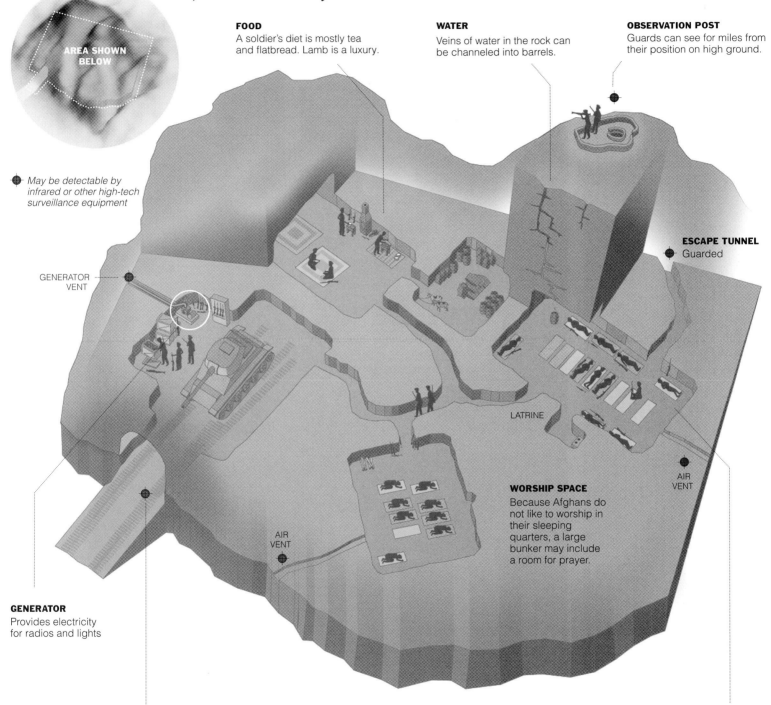

AREA SHOWN BELOW

FOOD
A soldier's diet is mostly tea and flatbread. Lamb is a luxury.

WATER
Veins of water in the rock can be channeled into barrels.

OBSERVATION POST
Guards can see for miles from their position on high ground.

May be detectable by infrared or other high-tech surveillance equipment

GENERATOR VENT

ESCAPE TUNNEL
Guarded

LATRINE

AIR VENT

WORSHIP SPACE
Because Afghans do not like to worship in their sleeping quarters, a large bunker may include a room for prayer.

AIR VENT

GENERATOR
Provides electricity for radios and lights

ENTRANCE
Bunkers are often built with a rocky overhang above openings so they cannot be glimpsed in satellite pictures. All entrances and exits are guarded.

WEAPONS STORAGE
Weapons may include tanks, rocket-propelled grenades, multiple rocket-launchers, antiaircraft machine guns, rifles and smaller arms.

TEMPERATURE
Because a bunker is deep inside a mountain, it is protected from extreme weather. Even in winter, bunkers at low altitudes generally remain at 40 to 50 degrees.

SLEEPING QUARTERS
Soldiers sleep on the rock floor. A pit dug in the ground serves as a latrine.

Sources: Jack Shroder and Thomas E. Gouttierre, University of Nebraska at Omaha; Defense Department; U.S. Army Foreign Military Studies Office   HANNAH FAIRFIELD; ILLUSTRATION BY JOHN PAPASIAN/THE NEW YORK TIMES

U.S. Forces Defeat Taliban

POOL PHOTO BY BRENNAN LINSLEY

Crossing by air over the hills into Afghanistan from Tajikistan, American Special Operations soldiers keep watch from the open back end of an Army Special Forces Chinook helicopter. November 15, 2001.

The retreat of the Taliban has opened the next critical phase of the American campaign in Afghanistan: joining the effort to deliver relief for millions of hungry, cold, sick, war-weary Afghans. In the end, the war against famine, disease and misery may prove as important as the military campaign in ending a generation of misrule and chaos.

The military will be full partners in the mobilization now getting under way. NATO allies will ship food, clothing, shelter and medicine to the nations surrounding Afghanistan for United Nations relief organizations, private aid groups and intrepid Afghan truckers to deliver to people in ruined cities and shattered villages. The United States is buying millions of tons of wheat, much of it delivered in red, white and blue bags stamped USA, to help keep Afghans from starving this winter.

—**Tim Weiner**
NOVEMBER 16, 2001

POOL PHOTO BY DAVE MARTIN

*A Marine CH-53E Super Stallion helicopter flies over Camp Rhino
in southern Afghanistan. December 8, 2001.*

Life After the Fall of the Taliban

JAMES HILL FOR THE NEW YORK TIMES

Women wait for food to be distributed at a refugee camp in northern Afghanistan. October 1, 2001.

The Taliban imposed a harsh variety of Islam that brought them condemnation around the globe. All men had to wear beards at least four inches long. No woman could work or go to school or leave the house alone, and women had to be completely covered if they ventured out of their houses at all. Television and music and many other forms of recreation were banned.

Last week, men in the liberated cities had their beards trimmed. Women uncovered their faces and walked freely out of doors. People listened to music and brought their television sets out of hiding.

—**Staff**
NOVEMBER 18, 2001

The freedom is still too new to completely trust, and the wounds too fresh to be healed, but for the first time in years, women here say they have hope — that they will be treated like human beings, not wayward cattle; that they will be free to leave their homes and work; that their daughters will be able to learn.

—**Amy Waldman**
NOVEMBER 19, 2001

Jamillah, who fled Afghanistan, holds her 10-month-old son, Shabanah, at the Doctors Without Borders clinic in the Jalozi refugee camp. Peshawar, Pakistan. November 6, 2001.

▶

STEPHEN CROWLEY/THE NEW YORK TIMES

At School and at Play

Haziza, a 12-year-old refugee from Afghanistan, sits in a first grade classroom with children much younger than she is. They raise their hands to answer a question she can't. Under Taliban rule in Afghanistan, Haziza was not allowed to go to school, and now, in Pakistan, she is struggling to make up for missed years of education. Peshawar, Pakistan. October 26, 2001.

RUTH FREMSON/THE NEW YORK TIMES

The years of Taliban rule have not only denied girls an education but boys as well. Their schools may have been open but very little teaching was going on. And when teaching did occur, religion very often replaced reading, writing and arithmetic in the curriculum.

—Barry Bearak
OCTOBER 30, 2001

Children at play in Kunduz, Afghanistan. December 23, 2001.

CHANG W. LEE/THE NEW YORK TIMES

RUTH FREMSON/THE NEW YORK TIMES

4
Meeting the Challenge at Home

◄ *Eight U.S. athletes carry the American flag during the opening ceremony of the 2002 Winter Olympics in Salt Lake City, Utah. The tattered flag was recovered from the World Trade Center site. February 8, 2002.*

CHANG W. LEE/THE NEW YORK TIMES

POOL PHOTO BY STAN HONDA

Fires caused by aftereffects of the collapse of the twin towers continued to burn for many weeks. Clouds of smoke make the work even more difficult at ground zero on October 11, 2001. Some 300 firefighters exposed to smoke and dust from the disaster were on leave for respiratory problems, as of January 2002.

Cleaning Up the Site

The excavators claw through the pile. The ironworkers are hoisted in a bucket to burn away the remaining wall. It rains fire, pressurized water dissipates into mist and the blowtorches produce an eerie green vapor. The pit fumes a white stinking smoke. Men shout. The falling metal makes the sound of the ocean booming as it breaks over the shore.

— **Charlie LeDuff**
SEPTEMBER 24, 2001

Cleanup of the site began almost immediately and operated 24 hours a day, 7 days a week. At any given time, 600 to 700 people worked at the site. The cleanup was completed on May 30, 2002; original estimates had been two to three years. As of April 8, 101,759 truckloads of debris, weighing 1,506,124 tons, had been removed, including 183,863 tons of steel. The cost of the cleanup is about $600 million, well below previous estimates of $2 billion.

POOL PHOTO BY TED S. WARREN

Workers carry buckets of debris out of the site. September 24, 2001.

On May 30, 2002, a ceremony marking the end of the recovery effort at ground zero took place.

BRAD LAPAYNE FOR THE NEW YORK TIMES

Safety in the Skies

Trying to soothe the frayed nerves of reluctant American travelers, President Bush announced today that the federal government would take on a larger role in airport security and that more than 4,000 National Guard troops would begin protecting the nation's 420 commercial airports within days.

In addition, the president said he would give grants to airlines to allow them to develop stronger cockpit doors and transponders that cannot be switched off from the cockpit. Government grants would also be available to pay for video monitors that would be placed in the cockpit to alert pilots to trouble in the cabin; and new technology, probably far in the future, allowing air traffic controllers to land distressed planes by remote control.

Mr. Bush also said his administration had ordered what he described as a major increase in the number of armed, plainclothes sky marshals on planes, although he would not provide numbers.

—Elisabeth Bumiller
SEPTEMBER 28, 2001

MONICA ALMEIDA/THE NEW YORK TIMES

In Los Angeles, California, when airports reopened after the attacks, travelers waited in long security checkpoint lines. September 14, 2001.

Canine Helpers

With little fanfare, bomb-sniffing dogs have become among the most effective, and important, security tools at airports, federal and local airport officials say. They work quickly and have an almost perfect record in separating real explosives from merely suspicious items — which has made them one of the best friends of harried travelers desperate to avoid the security delays that mar air travel.

While billions of dollars are being spent on devices that peek inside suitcases and carry-on bags, given the new federal mandates on screening all baggage, dogs offer reassurance and are far less intimidating than some of the new measures.

Officials in Los Angeles say the dogs may prove the salvation of travelers because they may do more to prevent unnecessary terminal evacuations and other security delays than many of the expensive new devices, like the massive CTX machines, which run a CAT scan of luggage. The Los Angeles airport has 13 of the machines — each weighs about 8,000 pounds and is roughly the size of a hefty sport utility vehicle — with more on the way.

"Where they really help the most is in that gray area, when we're asking, 'Should we or shouldn't we evacuate?'" Sergeant Blair Lindsay of the airport police said of the dogs. "They're so good. We always trust them."

"We chose these dogs in part because we want this," Sergeant Lindsay said. "People feel good around them."

"I don't know how the machines work," Sergeant Lindsay said. "Somehow I feel better knowing a brain is thinking about this and continually separating out the small things. I really have a lot of confidence in these dogs."

—**James Sterngold**
MARCH 21, 2002

In addition to working in airports, dogs were also a large help in the cleanup effort at ground zero. A volunteer, Jan Price, massages a German shepherd after his shift. September 14, 2001.

RUTH FREMSON/THE NEW YORK TIMES

STEVE BERMAN/THE NEW YORK TIMES

A bomb-sniffing dog and a Port Authority police officer examine unaccompanied baggage in a check-in line at LaGuardia Airport in New York. September 13, 2001.

Misplaced Anger

ANDRES SERRANO FOR THE NEW YORK TIMES
INTERVIEWS BY CATHERINE SAINT LOUIS
PUBLISHED ON SEPTEMBER 23, 2001

Mohammed Ayesh: "I work for a car service. When people get in, some — only a few — look at me with anger because of what happened. I don't blame them. Every human being falls into the same thing. They might have had relatives in the towers. But sometimes I blame them because it's not justified. Maybe I don't look like a white boy, but this tragedy hurt me, too."

The number of Muslims in the United States has generally been estimated to be as high as six million.

On September 12, more than 100 people, including many teenagers, held a march near a mosque in Bridgeview, Illinois, near Chicago. Some waved American flags and shouted "U.S.A.!"

Rafeeq Jaber, a board member of the Mosque Foundation in Bridgeview, said the marchers appeared to be "rallying against foreign nationals," not realizing many members of the mosque had been American citizens since before many of the marchers were born.

—**Laurie Goodstein and Gustav Niebuhr**
SEPTEMBER 14, 2001

JOHN ZICH/AGENCE FRANCE-PRESSE

A man hangs an American flag at the Mosque Foundation in
Bridgeview, Illinois. September 13, 2001.

As a Sikh man was trying to flee Lower Manhattan on Tuesday, he found himself running not only from flames, but also from a trio of men yelling invective about his turban.

—**Somini Sengupta**
SEPTEMBER 13, 2001

"It is un-Islamic to kill innocent people," said a 25-year-old Afghan police constable, Muhammad Anwar.

—**Barry Bearak**
SEPTEMBER 13, 2001

Coping With New Threats

The fires were still raging at ground zero — and a search for any survivors was under way — when public health officials in New York City sent out an urgent alert. The terrorist strike might not be over, the city warned hundreds of doctors and emergency rooms. An attack with anthrax spores, botulism, smallpox, even the plague, might well be next.

That warning — sent out before dawn on September 12 — turned out to be disturbingly prescient: the largest bioterrorism attack in United States history was about to begin. And before it would mysteriously peter out nearly three months later, five people would be dead and another 18 would have or would be suspected of having anthrax.

As the year came to a close and no new signs of anthrax-poisoned letters appeared, federal health officials privately expressed great relief. Yes, five people were dead; nearly 20 others became sick. But the bioterrorist nightmare that might have killed thousands turned out to be an epidemic that never happened. Calm slowly descended and reports of possible anthrax sightings stopped almost as quickly as they had started.

But this relatively isolated attack was more than enough to expose serious weaknesses in the public health response. A new national effort backed by billions in federal funds was started to better prepare the nation for any future bioterrorist assault. Local health departments, emergency room doctors and others had to be better trained. Millions of doses of anthrax antibiotics and smallpox vaccines were ordered for stockpiling. New laboratories had to be built to handle the deluge of samples that would need early testing in the event of a new scare.

—Eric Lipton
MARCH 7, 2002

MICHAEL SYPNIEWSKI FOR THE NEW YORK TIMES

Traces of anthrax were found in these mailboxes, outside the Princeton post office in West Windsor, New Jersey. October 28, 2001.

CHANG W. LEE/THE NEW YORK TIMES

A boatload of tourists departs Liberty Island after a terror threat on New York City landmarks, including the Statue of Liberty, is reported. May 21, 2002.

Federal and local law-enforcement officials yesterday issued a warning of vague and uncorroborated threats against the Brooklyn Bridge and the Statue of Liberty as the city imposed security measures not seen since the first months after the September 11 terrorist attacks.

When asked how people should respond to these warnings, Police Commissioner Raymond W. Kelly said, "People should take this in the sense that the government is reacting to information, doing what it thinks is prudent, and they should continue to go forward with their lives."

—**Dan Barry and Al Baker**
MAY 22, 2002

A Final Farewell

TYLER HICKS/THE NEW YORK TIMES

FRED R. CONRAD/THE NEW YORK TIMES

The recovery and cleanup efforts at the World Trade Center site ended on May 30, 2002. The last steel girder, draped in a black cloth and the American flag, was carried up a ramp out of the site. An empty stretcher with a flag on it was placed in an ambulance to symbolize those who were not recovered. The site of the former twin towers has become a construction site, as architects plan the buildings and memorials that will replace the World Trade Center.

How to Help

Some time has passed since the events of September 11, 2001. The dust has begun to settle in more ways than one. On May 30, 2002, the recovery site at the World Trade Center in New York City was officially closed. The workers have gone home, the machines have stopped, and now a silence remains to remind us of what was. The dust has also settled in most of our lives. We have all tried to move on — your parents have gone back to work, you have gone back to school, and we have mourned the victims of this tragedy. But the memories of what we witnessed have not left us. Thoughts still remain and resonate within each of us, but with those thoughts have come a sense of responsibility and unity among Americans.

The immediate outpouring of help that you see chronicled in this book has been followed by many months of ongoing support. Families of the victims continue to receive help, counseling and monetary support. There are flags flown high, and posters in New York City proclaim "I ♥ NY More Than Ever." People travel to Lower Manhattan to support the businesses there by shopping and eating in restaurants. And, of course, many thousands of people come from all over the world to visit the area and to spend a moment remembering the people who lost their lives.

We are a nation shaken by what happened, but we are a nation made stronger, too. Our airplanes are more secure, our national landmarks more closely watched. And although we went to war as a result of the attacks, the people of Afghanistan are no longer living under a brutally oppressive government. There is also a new global awareness about terrorism and what needs to be done to stop it.

With a renewed sense of purpose and hope for the future, America has turned its attention to both creating a memorial to the victims of the attacks and planning new construction on the site of ground zero. We have overcome the initial shock of this tragedy, and the sense of patriotism has never been stronger.

MARILYNN K. YEE/THE NEW YORK TIMES

Children at Public School 138 Annex in Crown Heights, Brooklyn, donate small change to the American Red Cross to help victims of the World Trade Center attack. The children started collecting the money in mid-September and raised about $200. November 7, 2001.

There are still many things you can do to help America and its people:

• Learn about other cultures. Go to the library and take out a book to help you understand the different nationalities and religions of your peers.

• Make friends with someone who looks different from you. Show others that racial and religious tolerance is very American.

• Plant a tree, make a mural, or just take a moment to reflect, to commemorate those people who lost their lives.

• Write letters to your local firefighters, police officers, and emergency workers to show your continued appreciation for the heroic work they do.

• Write letters to your local Congressional representative, Senator or to the President. Tell them how you feel about being an American.

— **The editors of Scholastic Nonfiction, with Adele Brodkin, Ph.D., Senior Child Development Consultant**

The Lower 48 States of the U.S.

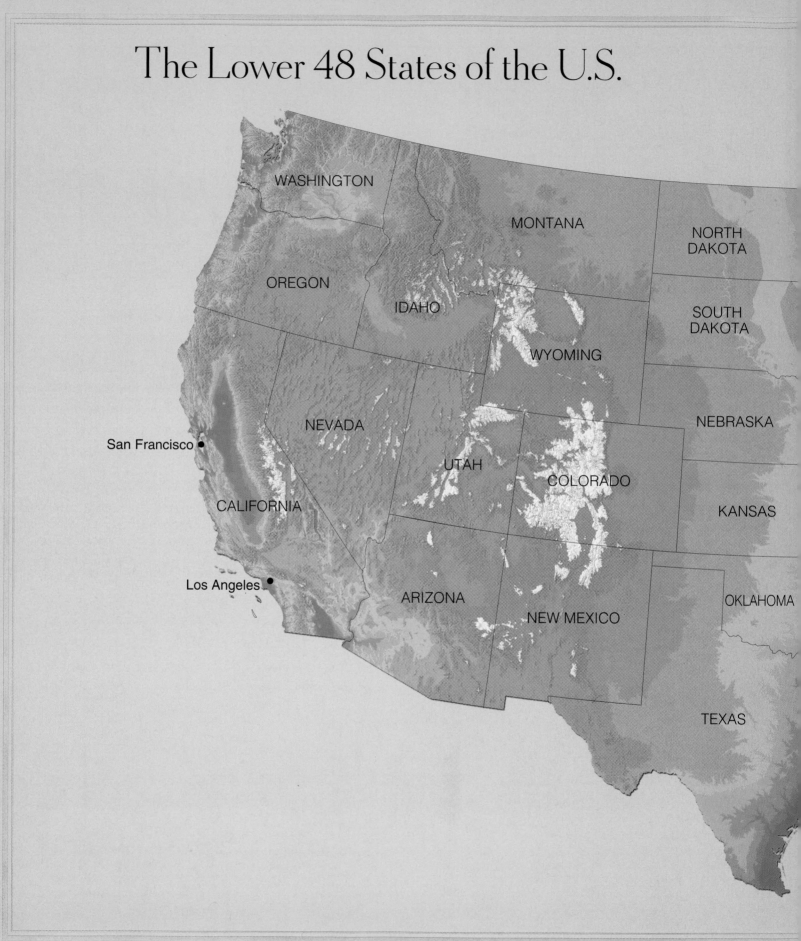

WASHINGTON

MONTANA

NORTH DAKOTA

OREGON

IDAHO

SOUTH DAKOTA

WYOMING

NEVADA

NEBRASKA

San Francisco

UTAH

COLORADO

CALIFORNIA

KANSAS

Los Angeles

ARIZONA

NEW MEXICO

OKLAHOMA

TEXAS

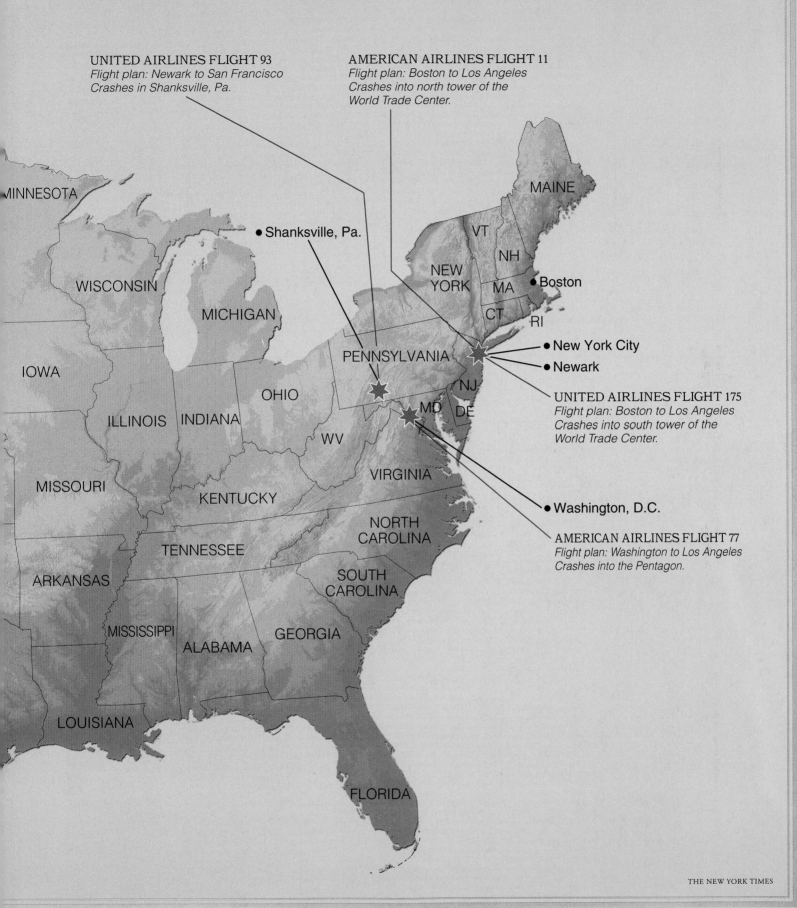

UNITED AIRLINES FLIGHT 93
Flight plan: Newark to San Francisco
Crashes in Shanksville, Pa.

AMERICAN AIRLINES FLIGHT 11
Flight plan: Boston to Los Angeles
Crashes into north tower of the
World Trade Center.

MINNESOTA

MAINE

● Shanksville, Pa.

VT

NH

WISCONSIN

NEW
YORK

MA

● Boston

MICHIGAN

CT

RI

IOWA

PENNSYLVANIA

● New York City

● Newark

OHIO

NJ

UNITED AIRLINES FLIGHT 175
Flight plan: Boston to Los Angeles
Crashes into south tower of the
World Trade Center.

ILLINOIS

INDIANA

MD

DE

WV

MISSOURI

KENTUCKY

VIRGINIA

● Washington, D.C.

NORTH
CAROLINA

AMERICAN AIRLINES FLIGHT 77
Flight plan: Washington to Los Angeles
Crashes into the Pentagon.

TENNESSEE

ARKANSAS

SOUTH
CAROLINA

MISSISSIPPI

GEORGIA

ALABAMA

LOUISIANA

FLORIDA

THE NEW YORK TIMES

Afghanistan

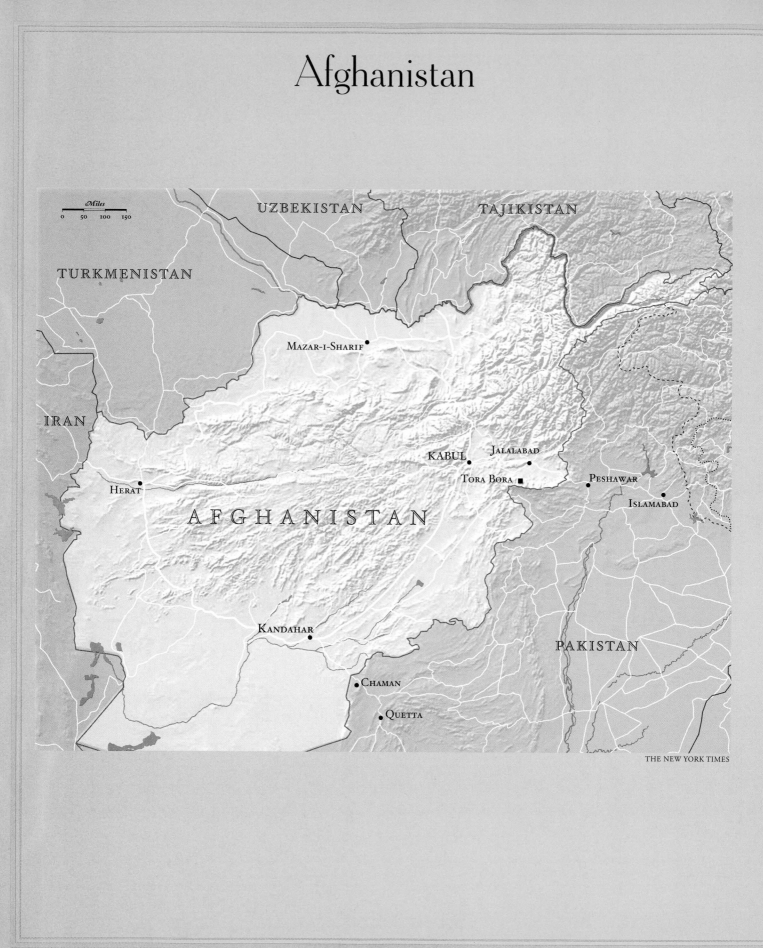

THE NEW YORK TIMES

Resources

The complete text and photographs of *The New York Times* coverage of the events of September 11, 2001, and its aftermath, including the Portraits of Grief, can be accessed at www.nytimes.com.

The following Web sites have bibliographies of books and other resources for children, young adults and adults. Each was written by children's book professionals.

American Booksellers Association
www.bookweb.org/news/btw/5042.html

Association for Library Service for Children
www.ala.org/alsc/dealing_with_tragedy.html

Children's Book Council (CBC)
www.cbcbooks.org/html/cbc_booklist.html

Educators for Social Responsibility
www.esrmetro.org

National Association for the Education of Young Children
www.naeyc.org/coping_with_disaster.htm

Young Adult Library Services Association
www.ala.org/yalsa/professional/traglist.html

Glossary

accelerate — to go faster and faster

aerial refuelers — airplanes carrying gasoline that refuel other airplanes while in the air

aftermath — result

Al Qaeda — *see* Qaeda

amphibious — able to travel or live on land and in water

anthrax — an infectious disease which can be fatal and is caused by spore-forming bacteria

antibiotic — a drug, such as penicillin, that kills bacteria and is used to cure infection and disease

aviation analyst — one who carefully examines the science of building and flying aircraft

balm — something that provides comfort

battalion — a large military unit

besiege — to cause worry or distress

bioterrorism — use of deadly bacteria to kill people or as a threat to force them to obey

botulism — a serious disease caused by bacteria in food that can result in paralysis

buckle — bend, give way or crumble

CAT scan — a tube that rotates around a person or an object and takes X rays

catastrophically — suddenly and terribly

chaos — total confusion

chaplain — a priest, minister or rabbi who works with an organization like the military, fire department or a hospital. A chaplain leads religious services and counsels people.

Chelsea Piers — a sports and entertainment complex in New York City

choreograph — to arrange and direct the steps and details of an action or a series of actions

civilian — someone who is not a member of the armed forces

commodity — a product

converge — to come together

corrugated — shaped into ridges or ripples

debris — the scattered pieces of something that has been broken or destroyed

defiance — standing up to someone or to some organization and refusing to obey

dissipate — to slowly go away or break apart

EMS — (abbreviation for Emergency Medical Services) people specially trained and licensed to provide rescue assistance and transportation to hospitals

ensue — to happen next

epidemic — the rapid spreading of a disease through a population

evacuation — an organized movement away from an area or a building

excavator — a truck with a shovel that lifts debris

F.A.A. — (abbreviation for Federal Aviation Administration) the government organization that regulates airlines

flatbread — thin bread made without yeast

force — strength or power

gallant — brave and fearless

harrowing — frightening

hijack — to take illegal control of a plane or other vehicle

homage — respect

in memoriam — in memory of

indiscriminate — random

inferno — a fire with intense heat

infrared — a form of light we cannot see; often used to locate structures

invective — insult

Islam — the religion based on the teachings of Mohammad

kamikaze — a person who makes a suicide crash into a target

Koran — (also spelled Qur'an) the holy book of the Islamic religion

laden — carrying a lot of something

lateral — on, from or to the side

latrine — a hole in the earth used as a toilet

load — force, strength or power

mar — spoil

MASH — (abbreviation for Mobile Army Surgical Hospital) temporary hospitals set up close to the front lines in a war zone

mayoral — for the mayor, leader of a town or city government

memorial — something that is built or done to help people continue to remember a person or an event

militants	people prepared to fight for, or be very aggressive in support of, a cause in which they believe
mosque	a building used by Muslims for worship
Muslim	someone who follows the religion of Islam
NATO	(abbreviation for North Atlantic Treaty Organization) a military alliance consisting of many countries. Each member country agrees to treat an attack on any other member as an attack on itself.
obliterate	to destroy something completely
ornery	stubborn
orthodox	belief in the more traditional teachings of a religion
Pentagon	a five-sided building in Arlington, Virginia, that is the headquarters of the U.S. Department of Defense
perpetrator	someone who commits a crime
plague	a very serious disease that spreads quickly to many people and often causes death
plummet	to fall straight down quickly
Port Authority (of New York and New Jersey)	
	an organization that operates the major airports, shipping ports, bus terminals, and bridges and tunnels in the New York City area
prescient	to know in advance
primary election	an election to choose a party candidate who will run in the general election
prudent	cautious and careful
Qaeda (Al)	a militant organization that supports Muslim fighters in several countries. It also trains members of terrorist organizations.
radar	a device set up to track the route of planes using radio waves
reconnaissance aircraft	
	military airplanes sent out to do a preliminary survey of enemy territory
refugee	a person who is forced to leave his or her home because of war, persecution, famine or natural disaster

resolve	determination
rubble	broken pieces of buildings
Salvation Army	an international religious and charitable organization that helps those in need
scores	a large number
screen	to examine carefully in order to make a selection or to separate into groups
shrine	a place to honor a person, religious figure or historical event
[sic]	indicates that the word before it is reproduced exactly as printed in the original document
Sikh	a member of a religious sect of India that believes in a single god
sky marshals	men and women who ride in airplanes to watch for people who break the law
smallpox	a very contagious and sometimes deadly disease that causes chills, high fever and sores that can leave permanent scars
spontaneous	without previous thought or planning
surveillance	close observation
Taliban	a religious movement that demands very strict following of Islam, including not allowing women to work outside the home or appear in public without being fully covered, requiring men to wear full beards, and banning most forms of nonreligious entertainment, including music, movies, TV and dance. It controlled most of Afghanistan from 1995 until 2002.
thwart	stop
transponder	a device in an airplane that sends and receives radar signals from air traffic control centers
traumatize	suffering from a severe and painful emotional shock
truss	a group of beams forming a framework of a building
uncorroborated	unconfirmed
vaccine	a substance containing dead, weakened or living organisms that can be injected or taken orally. A vaccine causes a person to produce antibodies that protect him or her from the disease caused by the organisms.
virtually	nearly or almost

Index

Compilation copyright © 2002 by The New York Times Company and Callaway Editions, Inc.

All rights to individual works are reserved by the artist, The New York Times, or, if applicable, the organization credited. Every effort has been made to trace the ownership of every selection included, to secure the necessary permission to reprint the selection, and to make full acknowledgment for its use. In the event of any question arising as to the right to use any material, the publisher, while expressing regret for any inadvertent error, will be happy to make the necessary correction in any future printings, provided notification is sent to the publisher. Published by Scholastic Inc. in association with The New York Times Company and Callaway Editions, Inc. SCHOLASTIC, SCHOLASTIC NONFICTION, and associated logos are trademarks and/or registered trademarks of Scholastic Inc. The New York Times and The New York Times logotype, and Callaway and the Callaway logotype, and Callaway Editions, Inc., are trademarks.

Some additional text from The Scholastic Children's Dictionary © 2002, 1996 by Scholastic Inc.

No part of this publication may be reproduced, or stored in a retrieval system, or transmitted in any form or by any means, electronic, mechanical, photocopying, recording, or otherwise, without written permission of the publisher.
For information regarding permission, write to Scholastic Inc., Attention: Permissions Department, 557 Broadway, New York, NY 10012.

Library of Congress Cataloging-in-Publication Data available.

0-439-48803-6

10 9 8 7 6 5 4 3 2 1   02 03 04 05 06

Printed in the U.S.A.
First printing, September 2002

Visit Callaway at www.callaway.com
Visit The New York Times at www.nytimes.com
Visit Scholastic Inc. at www.scholastic.com

Produced by Callaway Editions, Inc.

Nicholas Callaway, Editorial Director
Antoinette White, Senior Editor • Sarina Vetterli, Assistant Publisher • George Gould, Production Director
Toshiya Masuda, Art Director • Masako Ebata, Assistant Designer
Carol Hinz, Associate Editor • Ivan Wong Jr. and José Rodríguez, Design and Production
With many thanks to Barbara Marcus, Jean Feiwel, Kenneth Wright, Kate Waters, Danielle Denega
and Karen Capria at Scholastic Inc., and Phyllis Collazo, Merrill Perlman and Peter Edidin at The New York Times.

Front cover photographs, clockwise from top left: Edward Keating/The New York Times, Lonnie Schlein/The New York Times, Suzanne DeChillo/The New York Times, James Estrin/The New York Times, Chang W. Lee/The New York Times, Krista Niles/The New York Times, Richard Perry/The New York Times, Linda Spillers
Back cover photograph by Vincent Laforet/The New York Times

FRED R. CONRAD/THE NEW YORK TIMES, PAUL MYODA, JULIAN LAVERDIERE

Cover image of The New York Times Magazine.
September 23, 2001.

After September 11, *The New York Times Magazine* asked the artists Julian LaVerdiere and Paul Myoda to create an image that could be used on the cover of the September 23, 2001, issue, which was to be devoted entirely to the tragedy. This image, developed by them and the *Times* photographer Fred R. Conrad, was the result.

On March 11, 2002, two actual beams of light soared into the night sky near the World Trade Center site, memorializing the loss of the twin towers and all those who perished in the terrorist attack. This "Tribute in Light," shown on the back cover, made real the image first conceived for the September 23 magazine cover and included the efforts of other artists who had also been working on a similar idea.

J303.625
N

**The East Hartford
Public Library**

Class J303.625 No. _____

Accession No. 09-265 _____

GAYLORD M

EAST HARTFORD PUBLIC LIBRARY

3 2523 11471 5280

DISCARD